INTELLIGENCE

WITHOUT AMBITION

IS A BIRD

WITHOUT WINGS.

IT IS HARD
FOR AN EGG
TO TURN INTO
A BIRD,
BUT IT IS HARDER
FOR IT TO LEARN
TO FLY
WHILE REMAINING AN EGG.

WE ARE LIKE EGGS
AND YOU CANNOT GO ON
BEING
JUST AN ORDINARY,
DECENT EGG.
YOU MUST BE HATCHED
OR GO BAD.

A forest bird
never
wants a cage

JUST AS THE BIRD
SINGS
OR THE BUTTERFLY
SOARS,
BECAUSE IT IS
HIS NATURE,
SO THE ARTIST
WORKS.

FAITH
IS THE BIRD
THAT FEELS
THE LIGHT
WHEN THE DAWN
IS STILL
DARK.

The   soul

has

illusions

as

the

bird

has wings

A BIRD DOESN'T SING
BECAUSE IT HAS AN ANSWER,
IT SINGS BECAUSE
IT HAS A SONG.

EVERYONE KNOWS BIRDS.
WHAT WILD CREATURE
IS MORE ACCESSIBLE
TO OUR EYES AND EARS,
AS CLOSE TO US
AND EVERYONE
IN THE WORLD,
AND AS UNIVERSAL
AS A BIRD?

FOR iN MUCH WISDOM iS MUCH GRIEF AND HE THAT iNCREASETH KNOWLEDGE iNCREASETH SORROW.

IF I WERE A BIRD
I WOULD FLY
ABOUT THE EARTH
SEEKING
THE AUTUMNS.

LIKE BONES
TO THE HUMAN BODY,
LIKE AXLES TO THE WHEELS,
LIKE WINGS TO THE BIRD,
AND LIKE THE AIR TO THE WING,
SO IS LIBERTY
THE ESSENCE OF LIFE.

LITTLE DOVE,
BRING ME
YOUR LETTER.

PROBABLY
IT IS FROM
MY MOTHER,
BECAUSE I HAVE
WRITTEN TO HER.

LITTLE BIRD, FLY BACK AND
BRING A WINK TO MY MOTHER.
ONE DAY, WHEN I GET OLD, I WILL ACCOMPANY YOU.

THE HUMAN
BIRD
SHALL TAKE HIS FIRST
FLIGHT,
FILLING THE WORLD
WITH AMAZEMENT,
ALL WRITINGS
WITH HIS
FAME,
AND BRINGING
ETERNAL
GLORY
TO THE NEST
WHENCE HE SPRANG.

BE LIKE THE BIRD
WHO,
PAUSING
IN YOUR FLIGHT
AWHILE ON BOUGHS
TOO SLIGHT,
FEEL THEM
GIVE WAY
BENEATH YOU,
AND YET
SING,
KNOWING
YOU HAVE
WINGS.

If you cannot catch
a bird
of paradise,

better take a wet hen.

A LEAF
FLUTTERED IN
THROUGH MY WINDOW
THIS MORNING,
AS IF IT WAS SUPPORTED
BY THE RAYS
OF THE SUN,
AND A BIRD
SETTLED
ON THE FIRE ESCAPE,
SO I FOUND JOY
IN MY CUP OF COFFEE,
AND JOY
ACCOMPANIED ME
AS I WALKED.

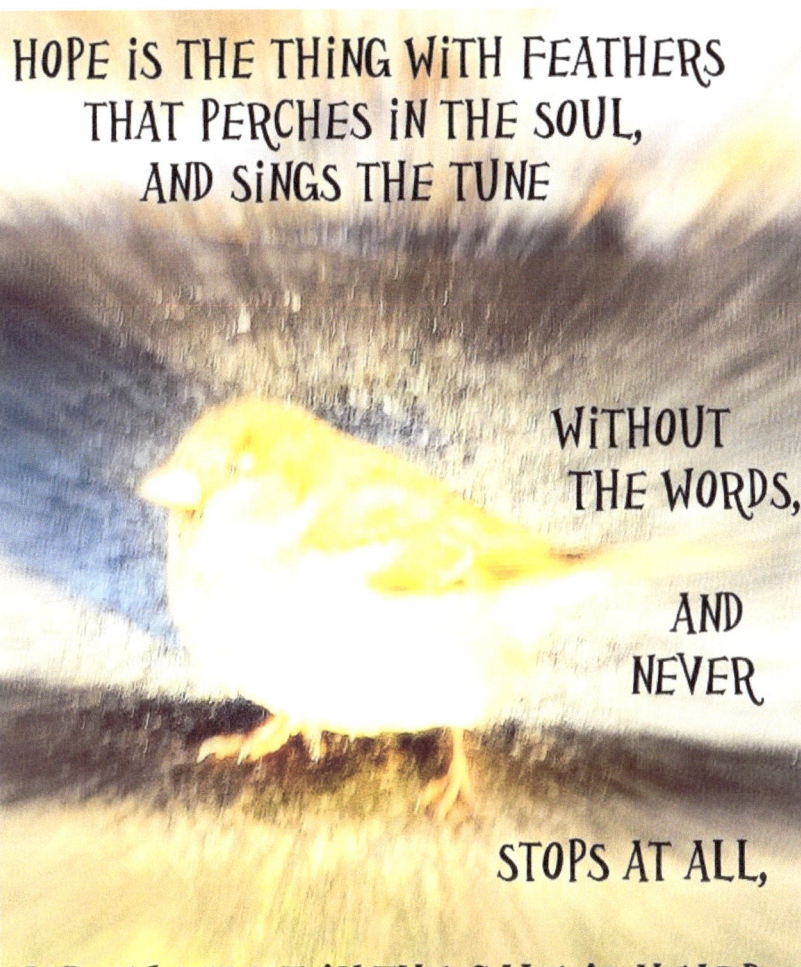

HOPE IS THE THING WITH FEATHERS
THAT PERCHES IN THE SOUL,
AND SINGS THE TUNE

WITHOUT
THE WORDS,

AND
NEVER

STOPS AT ALL,

AND SWEETEST IN THE GALE IS HEARD;
AND SORE MUST BE THE STORM
THAT COULD ABASH THE LITTLE BIRD
THAT KEPT SO MANY WARM.

WHEN
YOU HAVE SHOT
ONE BIRD
FLYING
YOU HAVE SHOT
ALL BIRDS
FLYING.
THEY ARE ALL
DIFFERENT
AND THEY FLY
IN DIFFERENT WAYS
BUT THE SENSATION
IS THE SAME
AND THE LAST ONE
IS AS GOOD
AS THE FIRST.

Morning

coffee

with my darling

BE AS A BIRD

PERCHED

ON A FRAIL BRANCH

THAT YOU FEEL BENDING

BENEATH YOU,

STILL YOU SING AWAY

ALL THE SAME,

KNOWING

YOU HAVE WINGS.

WHEN YOU HAVE SEEN
ONE ANT,
ONE BIRD,
ONE TREE,
YOU HAVE NOT SEEN
THEM ALL.

THE GREATEST ACHIEVEMENT
WAS AT FIRST
AND FOR A TIME
A DREAM.
THE OAK
SLEEPS IN THE ACORN,
THE BIRD
WAITS IN THE EGG,
AND IN THE HIGHEST VISION
OF THE SOUL
A WAKING ANGEL STIRS.
DREAMS
ARE THE SEEDLINGS
OF REALITIES.

The soul
    has illusions

as the bird
    has wings

IT'S BEST TO HAVE FAILURE HAPPEN
EARLY IN LIFE.
IT WAKES UP THE PHOENIX BIRD
IN YOU

FAITH
WITHOUT WORKS
IS LIKE A BIRD
WITHOUT WINGS;
THOUGH YOU MAY HOP
WITH YOUR COMPANIONS
ON EARTH,
YET YOU WILL NEVER
FLY WITH THEM
TO HEAVEN.

UTTERLY GONE
OUT OF THE WORLD
IS THE SONG
OF A DESTROYED
WILD BIRD.

MAN CAN FLY
IN THE AIR
LIKE A BIRD,
SWIM
UNDER THE OCEAN
LIKE A FISH,
HE CAN BURROW
INTO THE GROUND
LIKE A MOLE.
NOW
IF ONLY HE COULD
WALK THE EARTH
LIKE A MAN,
THIS WOULD BE
PARADISE.

MY

BONNIE

LIES

OVER

THE

OCEAN

Animal Peculiarity Part 7

By T.P Just

~~~

Get All The Books In The Series:

Animal Peculiarity Part 1
Animal Peculiarity Part 2
Animal Peculiarity Part 3
Animal Peculiarity Part 4
Animal Peculiarity Part 5
Animal Peculiarity Part 6
Animal Peculiarity Part 7
Animal Peculiarity Part 8
Just Enterprises

Table of Contents